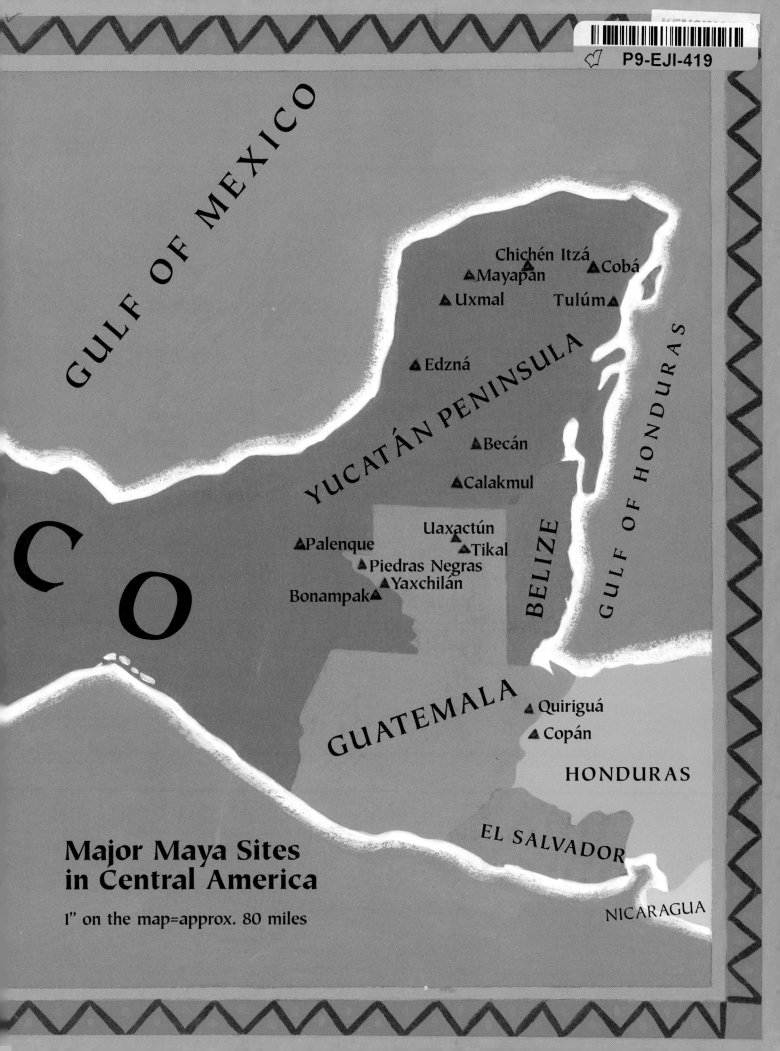

GULF OF MEXICO

Chichén Itzá
▲Mayapán ▲Cobá
▲ Uxmal Tulúm▲

▲ Edzná

YUCATÁN PENINSULA

▲Becán

▲Calakmul

Uaxactún
▲Palenque ▲
▲Tikal
▲ Piedras Negras
▲Yaxchilán
Bonampak▲

BELIZE

GULF OF HONDURAS

C

O

GUATEMALA

▲ Quiriguá
▲ Copán

HONDURAS

EL SALVADOR

NICARAGUA

Major Maya Sites
in Central America

1" on the map=approx. 80 miles

GODS AND GODDESSES
OF THE ANCIENT MAYA

GODS AND GODDESSES OF THE ANCIENT MAYA

Leonard Everett Fisher

HOLIDAY HOUSE / NEW YORK

To my grandchildren—

Samuel Benjamin Plotner
Gregory Byron Fisher
Jordan Lucas Plotner
Lauren Nicole Aldoroty
Danielle Olivia Fisher
Michael Steven Aldoroty

with love

Library of Congress Cataloging-in-Publication Data
Fisher, Leonard Everett.
Gods and goddesses of the ancient Maya / Leonard Everett Fisher.
p. cm.
Includes bibliographical references.
Summary: Gives the history of the principal gods and goddesses of the ancient Mayans,
including Hunab Ku, Itzamná, Ix Tab, and Ah Puch.
ISBN 0-8234-1427-2
1. Maya gods Juvenile literature. 2. Maya goddesses Juvenile literature. 3. Mayas—
Religion Juvenile literature. [1. Mayas—Religion. 2. Indians of Central America—Religion.]
I. Title. F1435.3.R3F47 1999 99-19900
299'.73—dc21 CIP

INTRODUCTION

Anthropologists who study the origin of tribes and ethnic groups date the appearance of the people who would become the Maya in the Americas at about 15,000 years ago. There are some recent genetic tests that suggest that two unrelated groupings of peoples became the first Americans: some may have originated in Asia and probably crossed a land bridge to America; the others might have been of Eurasian background and arrived in the Americas by unknown means.

Descendants of the group that might have been of Eurasian background, the Maya, may have emigrated northward from South America, where they had been living, and moved into the sweltering lowlands of the area that is now Guatemala. By 200 C. E. Maya civilization was flourishing in Mesoamerica.

The Mayas stood out from other cultures of the region, and indeed of the world, in many ways. They developed sophisticated systems of mathematics and writing that distinguished them from most other peoples. Unlike the Egyptians, Greeks, and Arabs, who profited from one another's cultures, the Maya seem to have developed large parts of their systems on their own— a remarkable accomplishment, especially given the incredible accuracy of their mathematical calculations.

Maya priests already had knowledge of mathematics and measurements by 200 C. E. Their skill at calculations enabled them to build stone temples, pyramids, astronomical observatories, and other dramatic-looking buildings. Around these structures grew great city-states, such as Chichén Itzá, Tikal, Uxmal, Uaxactún, and Copán. These cities became the heart and soul of Maya power. Here nobles governed and priests called upon gods and goddesses to protect and defend their people.

Although Maya nobles held political power, Maya priests may have been the true center of Maya civilization. It was the priests who developed the *vigesimal* mathematical system. This system is based on twenty units, unlike our *decimal* system's ten, and was one of the few in the world to include the concept of zero. The priests observed the heavens carefully, tracking the planets, comets, eclipses, and the rising and setting of both the sun and the moon. They were so adept at these measurements that they came up with a year of 365 days—off by only the smallest amount from what today's scientists measure!

The Maya also developed a sophisticated written language. Unlike our written language, which reflects only sounds, their written language was similar to the Egyptian hieroglyphs in that some symbols represented sounds and others stood for whole words. The Maya used symbols—dots, bars, and pictures—called glyphs that communicated their ideas, opinions, rituals, rules, and religious beliefs. These glyphs were recorded on walls and in stone, wood, pottery, or on tree bark paper.

Classic Maya culture reigned from roughly 200 c. e. to 900 c. e. in the area of present-day Guatemala, Belize, parts of Honduras, and parts of Mexico. During its greatest period some several million Maya lived there. After that time, wars, drought, internal strife, and diseases shattered the empire and decimated the population. Only about 2 million Maya remained when the Spanish arrived in 1519.

ITZAMNÁ
God of All

Itzamná, son of Hunab Ku, the god of creation, was the chief god of the Maya. He was the god of day and night and presided over the heavens. Itzamná invented many important things, such as writing, mathematics, and the Maya calendar. He also divided the land of the Maya among the people and named each village, town, and city.

When he chose, Itzamná became the god of the sun or the moon. At other times he replaced Chac, the god of rain, and assumed his power. Itzamná could become anything or anyone he wanted to be. But he refused to have anything to do with destruction—wars, death, or sacrifices. This well-meaning, kind-hearted god brought learning, healing, and happiness to the Maya.

KINICH AHAU

God of the Sun

Kinich Ahau was the god of the sun, of day.
In many areas of ancient Maya, he was not
considered a completely separate god, but was
Itzamná, the god of all, when he appeared as
the sun god. In some villages and towns of the
northern Yucatán, however it was Kinich Ahau
who was worshiped as the chief god, the son of
Hunab Ku, not Itzamná.

Kinich Ahau shared many of Itzamná's traits.
He was a friendly god, one who brought good
health and happiness to his people. He, too,
would have nothing to do with the dark side
of life—sickness, anger, famine, disasters. To the
Maya, nighttime was filled with danger, while
daytime promised safety. They worshiped
Kinich Ahau for what he was—the sun—and
thanked him for his warmth, his light, and the
well-being he gave his people.

CHAC

God of Rain

Chac was the god of rain. With his long nose and
fanglike teeth, Chac could look ferocious. But
like Kinich Ahau, the sun, he was a benevolent
and kindly god.

As the god of rain, Chac was also the god of
fertility. He brought life-giving water to the world
and caused everything on the earth to grow.

Chac was actually four gods in one—one
for each region: the north, east, south, and west.
This meant that Chac could protect every part
of the land of the Maya—not one area would be
overlooked. To distinguish each of the four
parts of Chac, the Maya assigned them names
and colors. North was Zac Xib Chac (white);
east was Chac Xib Chac (red); south was Kan Xib
Chac (yellow); and west was Ek Xib Chac (black).

YUM KAAX
God of Corn

Yum Kaax, the god of corn, was as important a god as Chac, the god of rain. Maya life centered around corn. It was the staff of life, the staple food of the Maya. The success or failure of a corn crop truly meant the difference between life and death.

Like Chac, Yum Kaax was a life-giving god. He provided the seed from which corn grew and also protected the fields and farm animals. The Maya considered Yum Kaax generous and friendly. Like Itzamná and Kinich Ahau, he was a benevolent god. Yet unlike them, who were shown as toothless and old, Yum Kaax was portrayed as a young god, with an ear of corn growing out of his head.

KUKULCÁN
God of Wind

Through much of Maya history, the god of wind remained nameless. Since wind and rain so often come together, the wind god was always associated with Chac, the rain god. Some of the Maya felt that they were one and the same.

Yet after another people, the Aztecs, grew powerful, the Maya borrowed from their culture and made a distinction between the wind and the rain gods. They renamed Ehecatl, the Aztec wind god, Kukulcán. Kukulcán is also considered the Maya version of the great Aztec god, Quetzalcóatl.

EK CHUAH
God of War

Ek Chuah, the god of war, was a dark and frightening figure. Death was his constant companion. Sometimes he was painted completely black. At other times, his mouth would be painted a different color, usually a reddish brown. To emphasize his evil nature, the Maya portrayed him with a large, drooping lower lip.

Yet, Ek Chuah had another, more protective, side to him. He was a friend of merchants, especially those who were traveling from one village to another. Not only would he protect them from others, he would also guide them through the jungles and hillsides and see to it that they would not get lost, but would make it to their destinations.

XAMAN EK
God of the North Star

Xaman Ek was the North Star, the constant star that never moved from its place in the heavens. The ancient Maya distinguished north from south and east from west. They named each of these directional points: north was Xaman; east, Likin; south, Noho; and west, Chikin. The Maya established these points to aid travelers and improve their knowledge of astronomy, a field in which they were highly advanced.

The blunt-nosed god Xaman Ek protected travelers and was thought to be more trustworthy than the two-faced Ek Chuah, a sometime protector and sometime threat.

IX CHEL
Goddess of Childbirth

Ix Chel was wife of Itzamná, the god of all.
Her most important function was to protect
pregnant women and help them have healthy
babies. She invented weaving and taught that
skill to Maya women. When she was with her
husband, Ix Chel could be gentle and warm. If
he chose to become the god of the sun, she
would become the goddess of the moon.

However, most of the time Ix Chel was
viewed as a goddess of destruction. She made
floods wash away the corn crop, destroying the
fields and taking many human lives. In this
aspect, she was depicted with talonlike fingers
and toes and was adorned with human bones,
a serpent wriggling out of her head.

IX TAB

Goddess of Suicide

The Maya held a different view of death from most other peoples. To them, suicide, if properly done, could bring a person to a place without suffering. Ix Tab, as the goddess of suicide, would welcome to this place people who had led good lives and had hanged themselves. Those who had led evil lives or had committed suicide in another way were not welcomed by Ix Tab.

Also called the goddess of the gallows, Ix Tab was usually depicted as a dead woman, hanging from heaven with a rope around her neck. On her face and chest were black circles, the mark of death.

MANIK
God of Human Sacrifice

There is no benevolent side to Manik, the god of human sacrifice. Human sacrifice was a common ritual among the Maya. They would sacrifice people in the hopes that this would prevent the gods from visiting famine or destruction upon the people.

In their most elaborate ritual, a noble warrior, taken in battle, would be stretched on his back over a stone altar by four priests. Another priest would plunge a knife into his chest and tear out his heart. Manik would claim another victim.

BOLONTIKU
God of the Lower World

The Maya believed there were both upper and lower worlds. The lower world was a series of nine separate layers, which together were called Bolontiku. Each layer was ruled by a Bolontiku, so there were nine gods in one. Ah Puch, the god of death, resided in the lowest layer.

The upper world consisted of thirteen separate layers, which were presided over by Oxlahuntiku, who was actually both a single god and all thirteen in one.

PRONUNCIATION GUIDE

Ah Puch—(ah POOCH)—god of death

Bolontiku—(bo lo ti KOO)—god of the lower world

Chac—(CHAHK)—god of rain

Ek Chuah—(ek choo AH)—god of war

Hunab Ku—(hoo nahb KOO)—supreme being; creator of the Maya universe

Itzamná—(eets ahm NAH)—most important Maya god; god of all

Ix Chel—(eesh CHEL)—goddess of childbirth; wife of Itzamná

Ix Tab—(eesh TAHB)—goddess of suicide

Kinich Ahau—(keen eech ah AHW)—sun god

Kukulcán—(koo kool KAHN)—Maya name for Quetzalcóatl, god of wind

Manik—(mahn EEK)—god of human sacrifice

Oxlahuntiku—(osh la hoo tee KOO)—god of the upper world

Quetzalcóatl—(kets ahl KO aht)—Aztec god

Xaman Ek—(shah mahn EK)—god of the North Star

Yum Kaax—(yoom KAHSH)—god of corn

BIBLIOGRAPHY

Farb, Peter. *Man's Rise to Civilization*. New York: E. P. Dutton, 1968.

Fisher, Leonard Everett. *Calendar Art*. New York: Four Winds, 1987.

Gallenkamp, Charles. *Maya*. Third Revised Edition. New York: Viking, 1985.

Henderson, John. *The World of the Ancient Maya*. Ithaca, NY: Cornell University Press, 1981.

Morell, V. *Kennewick Man's Contemporaries*. Washington, DC: *Science*, vol. 280, April 10, 1998.

Morell, V. *Genes May Link Ancient Eurasians, Native Americans*. Washington, DC: *Science*, vol. 280, April 24, 1998.

Morley, Sylvanus G. *The Ancient Maya*. Palo Alto, CA: Stanford University Press, 1946.

Thompson, J. E. *Maya History and Religion*. Norman, OK: University of Oklahoma Press, 1976.

Valiant, George C. *Artists and Craftsmen in Ancient Central America*. Science Guide #88. New York: American Museum of Natural History, 1945.

The author would like to thank Brian Stross, Ph.D., Professor of Anthropology and Archaeology at the University of Texas at Austin for all his help.

MAYA NUMBERS

The Maya were remarkable mathematicians. Since they began by counting with their fingers *and* toes, their fine numbering system is based on twenty. The numbering system we use now, the Arabic, is based on ten—from counting fingers only. Yet the two systems are alike in a very important way. Both the Arabic and the Maya numbers include a symbol for zero.

The Maya numbering system only uses three symbols—a shell for zero, a dot for one unit, and a bar, for five units. It is how often these symbols are used and where they are placed that will tell you what a number is.

We have used the Maya numbers to show the page numbers of this book. Here are the numbers up to thirty-three.

| 0 | 1 | 2 | 3 | 4 |